How

You Can

Love

by Faith

BILL BRIGHT

CAMPUS CRUSADE FOR CHRIST

Building Spiritual Movements Everywhere

How You Can Love By Faith

Published by
Campus Crusade for Christ
375 Hwy 74 South, Suite A
Peachtree City, GA 30269

ISBN 978-1-56399-108-X

Design and typesetting by Genesis Publications.

Printed in the United States of America.

Unless otherwise indicated, Scripture quotations are taken from the *New International Version*, © 1973, 1978, 1984 by the International Bible Society. Published by Zondervan Bible Publishers, Grand Rapids, Michigan.

Scripture quotations designated TLB are from *The Living Bible*, © 1971 by Tyndale House Publishers, Wheaton, Illinois.

Scripture quotations designated NASB are from the *New American Standard Bible*, © 1960, 1962, 1963, 1968, 1971, 1972, 1975, 1977 by the Lockman Foundation, La Habra, California.

As a personal policy, Bill Bright has never accepted honorariums or royalties for his personal use. Any royalties from this book are dedicated to the glory of God and designated to the various ministries of Campus Crusade for Christ.

What Is a Transferable Concept?

When our Lord commanded the eleven men with whom He had most shared His earthly ministry to go into all the world and make disciples of all nations, He told them to teach these new disciples all that He had taught them (Matthew 28:18–20).

Later the apostle Paul gave the same instructions to Timothy: "The things you have heard me say in the presence of many witnesses entrust to reliable men who will also be qualified to teach others" (2 Timothy 2:2).

In the process of counseling and interacting with tens of thousands of students, laymen, and pastors since 1951, our staff have discovered the following:

* Many church members (including people from churches that honor our Lord and faithfully teach His Word) are not sure of their salvation.
* The average Christian is living a defeated and frustrated life.
* The average Christian does not know how to share his faith effectively with others.

In our endeavor to help meet these three basic needs and to build Christian disciples, Campus Crusade for Christ has developed a series of "how to's"—or "transferable concepts"—in which we discuss many of the basic truths that Jesus and His disciples taught.

A "transferable concept" is an idea or a truth that can be transferred or communicated from one person to another and then to another, spiritual generation after generation, without distorting or diluting its original meaning.

As these basic truths—"transferable concepts"—of the Christian life are made available through the printed word, films, video tapes, and audio cassettes in every major language of the world, they could well be used of God to help transform the lives of tens of millions throughout the world.

We encourage you to master each of these concepts by reading it thoughtfully at least six times[1] until you are personally prepared to communicate it to others "who will also be qualified to teach others." By mastering these basic materials and discipling others to do the same, many millions of men and women can be reached and discipled for Christ and thus make a dramatic contribution toward the fulfillment of the Great Commission in our generation.

Bill Bright

---

[1] Educational research confirms that the average person can master the content of a concept, such as this one, by reading it thoughtfully six times.

Contents

HOW YOU CAN LOVE BY FAITH

The Greatest Power Ever Known

The beautiful ballroom of the Marriott Hotel in Chicago was crowded to capacity with more than 1,300 college students and Campus Crusade staff. They seemed to hang on to every word as I explained one of the most exciting spiritual discoveries that I had ever made—how to love by faith.

For years I had spoken on the subject of love. I had a simple four-point outline:

1. God loves you unconditionally.
2. You are commanded to love others—God, your neighbors, your enemies.
3. You are incapable of loving others in your own strength.
4. You can love others with God's love.

But, as in the case of most sermons on love, something was missing. Then some years ago, in an early hour of the morning, I was awakened from a deep sleep. I knew that God had something to say to me. I felt impressed to get up, open my Bible, and kneel to read and pray. What I discovered during the next two hours has since enriched my life and the lives of tens of thousands of others. I had learned how to love.

With this discovery, God gave me the command to share this wonderful truth with Christians around the world. In that life-changing time of fellowship with the Lord, I was given a fifth point for my sermon on love—*we love by faith.*

Love is the greatest thing in the world—the greatest privilege and power known to man. Its practice in word and deed changed the course of history as the first-century Christians demonstrated a quality of life never before witnessed on this earth. The Greeks, Romans, Gentiles, and Jews hated one another. The very idea of love and self-sacrifice was foreign to their thinking. When they observed Christians from many nations, with different languages and cultures, actually loving one another and sacrificing to help each other, they responded in amazement, "Look how these Christians love one another!"[2]

I challenged the students at the conference to become part of a revolution of love. I suggested that they make a list of all the individuals they did not like and begin to love them by faith.

Early the next morning, a young woman with face aglow said to me, "My life was changed last night. For many years I have hated my parents. I haven't seen them since I was seventeen, and I am now twenty-two. I left home as a result of a quarrel five years ago and haven't written or talked to them since, although they have repeatedly encouraged me to return home. I determined that I would never see them again. I hated them.

"Before becoming a Christian a few months ago," she continued, "I had become a drug addict, a dope pusher, and a prostitute. Last night you told me how to love my parents, and I could hardly wait to get out of that meeting and call them. Can you believe it? I now really love them with God's kind of love and can hardly wait to see them!"

---

2 Robin Lane Fox, *Pagans and Christians* (San Francisco: Perennial Library, Harper and Row Publishers, 1986, 1988), p. 324. Crowds shouted this when Christians were brought to die in the Roman arenas.

Everybody wants to be loved. Most psychologists agree that man's greatest need is to love and be loved. No barrier can withstand the mighty force of love.

There are three Greek words translated into the one English word "love":

- *Eros*, which suggests sensual desire—it does not appear in the New Testament.
- *Phileo*, which is used for friendship or love of one's friends or relatives—it conveys a sense of loving someone because he is worthy of love.
- *Agape*, which is God's love: the purest, deepest kind of love—it is expressed not through mere emotions but as an act of one's will.

Agape is God's supernatural, unconditional love for you revealed supremely through our Lord's death on the cross for our sins. It is the supernatural love He wants to produce in you and through you to others, by His Holy Spirit. Agape love is given because of the character of the person loving rather than because of the worthiness of the object of that love. Sometimes it is love "in spite of" rather than "because of."

God underscores the importance of this kind of love through the inspired writing of the apostle Paul, as recorded in 1 Corinthians 13. In this beautiful and remarkable passage of Scripture, Paul writes that, apart from love, anything that you might do for God or others is of no value. Consider these words:

> *If I had the gift of being able to speak in other languages without learning them and could speak in every language there is in all of heaven and earth, but didn't love others, I would only be making noise.*
>
> *If I had the gift of prophecy and knew all about what is going to happen in the future, knew everything about everything, but didn't love others, what good would it do? Even if I had the gift of faith so that I could speak to a*

mountain and make it move, I would still be worth nothing at all without love.

If I gave everything I have to poor people, and if I were burned alive for preaching the Gospel but didn't love others, it would be of no value whatever (1 Corinthians 13:1–3, TLB).

In other words, no matter what you do for God and for others, it is of no value unless you are motivated by God's love.

Five Truths About Love

ut what is agape love? How does this kind of love express itself?

Paul gives us an excellent description:

Love is very patient and kind, never jealous or envious, never boastful or proud, never haughty or selfish or rude. Love does not demand its own way. It is not irritable or touchy. It does not hold grudges and will hardly even notice when others do it wrong.

It is never glad about injustice, but rejoices whenever truth wins out. If you love someone, you will be loyal to him no matter what the cost. You will always believe in him, always expect the best of him, and always stand your ground in defending him.

All the special gifts and powers from God will someday come to an end, but love goes on forever.

There are three things that remain—faith, hope, and love—and the greatest of these is love (1 Corinthians 13:4–8,13, TLB).

In the next chapter the apostle Paul, inspired by the Holy Spirit, admonishes: "Let love be your greatest aim" (1 Corinthians 14:1, TLB).

Let me share with you five vital truths about love that will help you understand the basis for loving by faith.

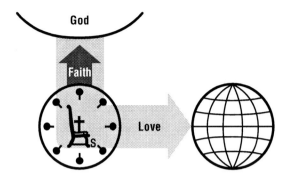

God Loves You Unconditionally

God loves with agape love, the love described in 1 Corinthians 13. He loves you so much that He sent His Son to die on the cross for you, that you might have everlasting life. His love is not based on performance. Christ loves you so much that, while you were yet a sinner, He died for you.

God's love for you is unconditional and undeserved. He loves you in spite of your disobedience, your weakness, your sin, and your selfishness. He loves you enough to provide a way to abundant, eternal life. From the cross Christ cried out, "Father, forgive them, for they do not know what they are doing" (Luke 23:34). If God loved those who are sinners that much, can you imagine how much He loves you—His child through faith in Christ and who seeks to please Him?

The parable of the prodigal son, as recorded in Luke 15, illustrates God's unconditional love for His children. A man's younger son asked his father for his share of the estate, packed his belongings, and took a trip to a distant land where he wasted all of his money on parties and prostitutes. About the time that his money was gone, a great famine swept over the land, and he began to starve. He finally came to his senses and realized that his father's hired men at least had food to eat. He decided, "I will go home to my father and say, 'Father, I have sinned against both heaven and you, and am no longer worthy of being called your son. Please take me on as a hired man'" (Luke 15:18, TLB).

While he was still a long distance away, his father saw him coming and was filled with loving compassion. He ran to his son, embraced him and kissed him. I think the reason he saw his son coming while he was still a long distance away was that he was praying for his son's return and spent much time each day watching that lonely road on which his son would return.

Even as the son was making his confession, the father interrupted to instruct the servants to kill the fatted calf and prepare for a celebration—his lost son had repented; he had changed his mind and had returned to become part of the family again.

God demonstrated His love for us before we were Christians, but this story makes it obvious that God continues to love His child who has strayed far from Him. He eagerly awaits his return to the Christian family and fellowship.

Even when you are disobedient, He continues to love you, waiting for you to respond to His love and forgiveness. Paul writes:

> *Since by his blood he did all this for us as sinners, how much more will he do for us now that he has declared us not guilty? Now he will save us from all of God's wrath to come. And since, when we were his enemies, we were brought back to God by the death of his Son, what blessings he must have for us now that we are his friends and he is living within us!* (Roman 5:9,10, TLB).

The love that God has for you is far beyond our human comprehension. Jesus prayed, "My prayer for all of them [the disciples and all future believers] is that they will be of one heart and mind, just as you and I are, Father…I in them and you in me, all being perfected into one—so that the world will know you sent me and will understand that *you love them as much as you love me*" (John 17:21,23, TLB).

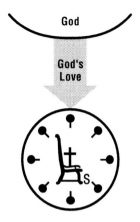

Think of it! God loves you as much as He loves His only begotten Son, the Lord Jesus. What a staggering, overwhelming truth to comprehend! You need have no fear of someone who loves you perfectly. You need never be reluctant to trust God with your entire life, for He truly loves you. And the almost unbelievable part of it is that He loves you even when you are disobedient.

Even on the human level, loving parents display such love. I loved my sons as much when they were disobedient as I did when they were good. For their sakes, because I do love them, I sometimes found it necessary to correct them. So it is in your relationship with God. When you are disobedient, He disciplines or corrects you because He loves you.

Hebrews 12 teaches about the love that motivates God's discipline:

> *Have you quite forgotten the encouraging words God spoke to you, his child? He said, "My son, don't be angry when the Lord punishes you. Don't be discouraged when he has to show you where you are wrong. For when he punishes you, it proves that he loves you..." Let God train you, for he is doing what any loving father does for his children. Whoever heard of a son who was never corrected?*

Since we respect our fathers here on earth, though they punish us, should we not all the more cheerfully submit to God's training so that we can begin really to live?

Our earthly fathers trained us for a few brief years, doing the best for us that they knew how, but God's correction is always right and for our best good, that we may share his holiness. Being punished isn't enjoyable while it is happening—it hurts! But afterwards we can see the result, a quiet growth in grace and character (Hebrews 12:5–7,9–11, TLB).

Christ's death on the cross has once and for all satisfied the wrath and justice of God for the believer's sin. God chastens and disciplines you to help you mature spiritually.

The early Christians endured persecution, hardships, and unbelievable suffering. Yet Paul wrote to them:

Who then can ever keep Christ's love from us? When we have trouble or calamity, when we are hunted down or destroyed, is it because he doesn't love us anymore? And if we are hungry or penniless or in danger or threatened with death, has God deserted us?

No, for the Scriptures tell us that for his sake we must be ready to face death at every moment of the day—we are like sheep awaiting slaughter; but despite all this, overwhelming victory is ours through Christ who loved us enough to die for us.

For I am convinced that nothing can ever separate us from his love. Death can't, and life can't. The angels won't, and all the powers of hell itself cannot keep God's love away. Our fears for today, our worries about tomorrow, or where we are—high above the sky, or in the deepest ocean—nothing will ever be able to separate us from the love of God demonstrated by our Lord Jesus Christ when he died for us (Romans 8:35–39, TLB).

Such love is beyond our ability to grasp with our minds, but it is not beyond our ability to experience with our hearts.

You Are Commanded to Love

A certain lawyer asked Jesus, "Sir, which is the most important command in the laws of Moses?"

Jesus replied, "'Love the Lord your God with all your heart, soul, and mind.' This is the first and greatest commandment. The second most important is similar: 'Love your neighbor as much as you love yourself.' All the other commandments and all the demands of the prophets stem from these two laws and are fulfilled if you obey them. Keep only these and you will find that you are obeying all the others" (Matthew 22:36–40, TLB).

At one time in my Christian life, I was troubled over the command to love God so completely. How could I ever measure up to such a high standard? Two very important considerations have helped me to desire to love and please Him completely.

First, the Holy Spirit has filled my heart with God's love, as promised in Romans:

> We know how dearly God loves us, and we feel this warm love everywhere within us because God has given us the Holy Spirit to fill our hearts with his love (Romans 5:5, TLB).

Second, by meditating on the attributes of God and the wonderful things He has done and is doing for me, I find my love for Him growing. I love Him because He first loved me (1 John 4:19).

How could God love me so much that He was willing to die for me? Why should God choose me to be His child? By what merit do I deserve to be His ambassador to tell this good news of His love and forgiveness to the world? On what basis do I deserve the privilege of His constant presence and His indwelling Spirit, of His promise to supply all of my needs according to His riches in glory? Why should I have the privilege—denied to most of the people of the world who do not know our Savior—of awaking each morning with a song in my heart and praise to Him on my lips for the love and joy and peace that He so generously gives to all who place their trust in His dear Son, the Lord Jesus?

I was a new Christian when I proposed to Vonette, who is now my wife. Although she had been an active church member, I discovered later that she was not a Christian at that time. Imagine her distress when, in my zeal for Christ, I explained to her that I loved God more than I loved her and that He would always be first in my life. I failed to explain, nor did I even realize at the time, that it was exactly because of my love for God that I was able to love her so much. Later, before we were married, she too experienced God's love and forgiveness and became His child.

Through the years He has become first in her life also, and because He is now first in each of our lives, we enjoy a much deeper love relationship than we could otherwise have known. Though my responsibilities in His service take me to many parts of the world and I am often away from her and our home, we both find our joy and fulfillment in Him. The times when we are privileged to be together are all the richer because of our mutual love for Him and His love for us.

The one who has not yet learned to love God and to seek Him above all else and all others is to be pitied, for that person is missing the blessings that await all who love God with all of their heart, soul, and mind.

It is natural for you to fulfill the command to love your neighbors as yourself if you truly love God with all of your heart, soul, and mind. If you are properly related to God on the vertical plane, you will be properly related to others on the horizontal plane.

For example, billiard balls, rolling freely on a table, naturally bounce away from each other because of the nature of their construction. But if we tie strings to several balls and lift them perpendicular to the table, the balls will cluster together.

When individual Christians are vitally yoked to Christ and related to God and are walking in the Spirit, loving Him with all of their hearts, souls, and minds, they will fulfill God's command to love others as themselves.

The apostle Paul explains:

If you love your neighbor as much as you love yourself you will not want to harm or cheat him, or kill him or steal from him. And you won't sin with his wife or want what is his, or do anything else the Ten Commandments say is wrong. All ten are wrapped up in this one, to love your neighbor as you love yourself. Love does no wrong to anyone. That's why it fully satisfies all of God's require-ments. It is the only law you need (Romans 13:9,10, TLB).

It is love for God and for others that results in righteous-ness, in fruit, and in glory to Christ.

Also, you are commanded to love others because such love testifies to your relationship with the Father. You demonstrate that you belong to Christ by your love for oth-ers. The apostle John practically equates your salvation with the way you love others when he says that if you don't love others, you do not know God, for He is love.

John says:

If someone who is supposed to be a Christian has money enough to live well, and sees a brother in need, and won't help him—how can God's love be within him? Little children, let us stop just saying we love people; let us really love them, and show it by our actions (1 John 3:17,18, TLB).

Jesus says:

I demand that you love each other as much as I love you (John 15:12, TLB).

As a Christian, you should love your neighbor because your neighbor is a creature of God made in the image of God; because God loves your neighbor; and because Christ died for your neighbor. Following the example of our Lord, you should love everyone, even as Christ did. You should devote your life to helping others experience His love and forgiveness.

Jesus also said:

"There is a saying, 'Love your friends and hate your enemies.' But I say: Love your enemies! Pray for those who persecute you! In that way you will be acting as true sons of your Father in heaven...

"If you love only those who love you, what good is that? Even scoundrels do that much. If you are friendly only to your friends, how are you different from anyone else? Even the heathen do that" (Matthew 5:43–47, TLB).

When Christians begin to act like Christians and love God, their neighbors, their enemies, and especially their Christian brothers—regardless of color, race, or class—we will see in our time, as in the first century, a great transformation in the whole of society. People will marvel when they observe our love in the same way people marveled when they observed those first-century believers saying, "How they love one another."

I counsel many students and older adults who are not able to accept themselves. Some are weighted down with guilt because of unconfessed sins; others are not reconciled to their physical handicaps. Still others feel inferior mentally or socially. My counsel to one and all is, "God loves you and accepts you as you are. You must do the same. Get your eyes off yourself! Focus your love and attention on Christ and on others. Begin to lose yourself in service for Him and for your fellow man."

God's kind of love is a unifying force among Christians. Paul admonishes us to "put on love, which is the perfect bond of unity" (Colossians 3:14, NASB) that our "hearts may be encouraged, having been knit together in love" (Colossians 2:2, NASB). Only God's universal love can break through the troublesome barriers that are created by human differences. Only a common devotion to Christ— the source of love—can relieve tension, ease mistrust, encourage openness, bring out the best in people, and enable them to serve Christ together in a more fruitful way.

One mother shared that the discovery of these principles enabled her to be more patient and kind to her husband and children. "The children were driving me out of my mind with all of their childish demands," she confided. "I was irritable with them, and because I was so miserable, I was a critical and nagging wife. No wonder my husband found excuses to work late at the office. It is all different now— God's love permeates our home since I learned how to love by faith."

A husband reported, "My wife and I have fallen in love all over again, and I am actually enjoying working in my office with men I couldn't stand before I learned how to love by faith."

You Cannot Love in Your Own Strength

Just as surely as "those who are in the flesh [the worldly, carnal[3] person] cannot please God," so in your own strength you cannot love as you should.

---

[3] The King James and New King James versions of the Bible use the term "carnal" in 1 Corinthians 3:3, "You are still *carnal*." Many modern versions render this passage differently: "You are still only baby Christians, *controlled by your own desires, not God's*" (TLB); "You are still *worldly*" (NIV); "You are still of the *flesh*" (RSV); "You are still *fleshly*" (NASB).

You cannot demonstrate agape love, God's unconditional love for others, through your own efforts. How many times have you resolved to love someone? How often have you tried to manufacture some kind of positive, loving emotion toward another person for whom you felt nothing? It is impossible, isn't it? In your own strength it is not possible to love with God's kind of love.

By nature people are not patient and kind. We are jealous, envious, and boastful. We are proud, haughty, selfish, and rude, and we demand our own way. We could never love others the way God loves us!

You Can Love With God's Love

It was God's kind of love that brought you to Christ. It is this kind of love that is able to sustain and encourage you each day. Through His love in you, you can bring others to Christ and minister to fellow believers as God has commanded.

God's love was supremely expressed in the life of Jesus Christ. You have a perfect, complete picture of God's kind of love in the birth, character, teachings, life, death, and resurrection of His Son.

How does this love enter your life? It becomes yours the moment you receive Jesus Christ and the Holy Spirit comes to indwell your life. The Scripture says, "We feel this warm love everywhere within us because God has given us the Holy Spirit to fill our hearts with his love" (Romans 5:5, TLB). God is Spirit and the "fruit of the Spirit is love..." (Galatians 5:22). When you are controlled by the Spirit, you can love with God's love.

When Christ comes into your life and you become a Christian, God gives you the resources to be a different kind of person. With the motivation, He also gives you the ability. He provides you with a new kind of love.

But how do you make love a practical reality in your life? How do you love? By resolutions? By self-imposed discipline? No. The only way to love is explained in my final point.

You Love By Faith

Everything about the Christian life is based on faith. You love by faith just as you received Christ by faith, just as you are filled with the Holy Spirit by faith, and just as you walk by faith.

If the fruit of the Spirit is love, you may logically ask, "Is it not enough to be filled with the Spirit?" This will be true from God's point of view, but it will not always be true in

your actual experience.

Many Christians have loved with God's love and have demonstrated the fruit of the Spirit in their lives without consciously or specifically claiming His love by faith. Yet, without being aware of the fact, they were indeed loving by faith; therefore, they did not find it necessary to claim God's love by faith as a specific act.

Hebrews 11:6 says, "Without faith it is impossible to please God." Obviously there will be no demonstration of God's love where there is no faith.

If you have difficulty in loving others, remember that Jesus has commanded, "Love each other just as much as I love you" (John 13:34, TLB). It is God's will for you to love. He would not command you to do something that He will not enable you to do. In 1 John 5:14,15, God promises that if you ask anything according to His will, He hears and answers you. Relating this promise to God's command, you can claim by faith the privilege of loving with His love.

God has an unending supply of His divine, supernatural, agape love for you. It is for you to claim, to grow on, to spread to others, and thus to reach hundreds and thousands with the love that counts, the love that will bring them to Jesus Christ.

In order to experience and share this love, you must claim it by faith; that is, trust His promise that He will give you all that you need to do His will on the basis of His command and promise.

This truth is not new. It has been recorded in God's Word for two thousand years. But it was a new discovery to me that early morning some years ago and, since that time, to many thousands of other Christians with whom I have shared it. When I began to practice loving by faith, I found that problems of tension with other individuals seemed to disappear, often miraculously.

In one instance, I was having a problem loving a fellow staff member. It troubled me. I wanted to love him. I knew that I was commanded to love him; yet, because of certain areas of inconsistency and personality differences, it was difficult for me to love him. But the Lord reminded me of 1 Peter 5:7, "Let him have all your worries and cares, for he is always thinking about you and watching everything that concerns you" (TLB). I decided to give this problem to Him and love this man by faith. When I claimed God's love for the man by faith, my concern lifted. I knew the matter was in God's hands.

An hour later, I found under my door a letter from that very man, who had no possible way of knowing what I had just experienced. In fact, his letter had been written the day before. The Lord had foreseen the change in me. This friend and I met together that afternoon and had the most wonderful time of prayer and fellowship we had ever experienced together. Loving with God's love by faith has changed our relationship.

Two gifted attorneys had great professional animosity, even hatred one for the other. Even though they were distinguished members of the same firm, they were constantly criticizing and making life miserable for each other.

One of the men received Christ through our ministry and some months later came for counsel.

"I have hated and criticized my partner for years," he said, "and he has been equally antagonistic toward me. But now that I am a Christian, I don't feel right about continuing our warfare. What shall I do?"

"Why not ask your partner to forgive you and tell him that you love him?" I suggested.

"I could never do that!" he exclaimed. "That would be hypocritical. I don't love him. How could I tell him I love him when I don't?"

I explained that God commands His children to love even their enemies and that His supernatural, unconditional agape love is an expression of our will, which we exercise by faith.

For example, the 1 Corinthians 13 kind of love is:

> ...very patient and kind, never jealous or envious, never boastful or proud, never haughty or selfish or rude. Love does not demand its own way. It is not irritable or touchy. It does not hold grudges and will hardly even notice when others do it wrong. It is never glad about injustice, but rejoices whenever truth wins out. If you love someone you will be loyal to him no matter what the cost. You will always believe in him, always expect the best of him, and always stand your ground in defending him (1 Corinthians 13:4–7, TLB).

"You will note," I explained, "that each of these descriptions of love is not an expression of the emotions, but of the will."

Together we knelt to pray and my friend asked God's forgiveness for his critical attitude toward his law partner and claimed God's love for him by faith.

Early the next morning, my friend walked into his partner's office and announced, "Something wonderful has happened to me. I have become a Christian. And I have come to ask you to forgive me for all that I have done to hurt you in the past, and to tell you that I love you."

His partner was so surprised and convicted of his own sin that he responded to this amazing confession by asking my friend to forgive him. Then to my friend's surprise, his partner said, "I would like to become a Christian, too. Would you show me what I need to do?"

After my friend showed him how through the *Four Spiritual Laws*, they knelt together to pray. Then they both came to tell me of this marvelous miracle of God's love.

A special assistant to a former governor of California once visited our headquarters at Arrowhead Springs, and during his visit he received Jesus Christ as Savior and Lord. He began to discover how to love by faith. His son had recently left home after they had had an argument. Contemplating the problem, this new Christian realized that he had never told his son that he loved him. On his way home, he asked the Lord to bring his son home so that he could make things right. He wanted to express his love for him. As he neared his home, his heart quickened. The upstairs light was on indicating that the son had come home! Soon, father and son embraced, became reconciled, and established a new relationship founded on God's forgiving love.

A young college football player, who had been raised in a community where blacks are resented, had always found it impossible to love blacks. One evening he heard me talk to a group of racially mixed students about loving by faith, especially in reference to loving those of other races.

"As you prayed," he told me later, "I claimed God's love for black people. Then, as I left the amphitheater, the first person I saw was a black man, and he was talking to a white girl. Now that is about as explosive a situation as you can imagine for a man who hates blacks. But suddenly I felt a compassion for that black man! At one time, I would have hated him and probably would have been rude and angry with him. But God heard my prayer."

That same evening a young black couple approached me. They were radiant.

"Something wonderful happened to me tonight," the young woman said. "I was liberated from my hatred for white people. I have hated whites since I was a little girl. I have known that as a Christian I should love white people, but I couldn't help myself. I hated whites and wanted to get revenge. Tonight I have begun to love whites by faith, and it really works."

The young man added, "It worked for me, too; now my hatred for whites is gone. Thank you for telling us how to love by faith."

Whites who have hated blacks and blacks who have hated whites have discovered God's supernatural love for each other. Christian husbands and wives who were living in conflict have claimed God's love by faith, and miracles have resulted. Parent-child struggles have been resolved and generation gaps have been bridged through loving by faith. Disputes in working situations have been resolved. Enemies cease to be enemies when you love them by faith. God's love has a way of dissolving prejudice and breaking down barriers.

Love is the greatest power known to man. It changed the course of the first-century world, and God is using it to bring a great revolution in the twentieth century. Nothing can overcome God's love.

In the first century there was a wedding of love and faith resulting in a great spiritual revolution throughout the

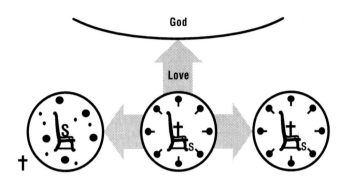

known world. Then both were lost during the Dark Ages. The realization of Martin Luther and his colleagues that the "just shall live by faith" ushered in the Reformation and another mighty movement of God's Spirit. But there was little love. It fact, there was often great conflict.

Today, God is bringing back to our remembrance the biblical wedding of the two—faith and love. Through faith, that supernatural, divine love of God will reach out where nothing else can go to capture men and women for Christ. The love which results from that faith will captivate people everywhere so that, as we live and love by faith, we will spread God's love throughout the world. This love is contagious, attractive, and aggressive. It creates hunger for God. It is active—constantly looking for loving things to do, people to uplift, and lives to change.

Leonard is an example. The night he received Christ as his personal Savior, his heart was filled with love, and a great change came over him. Until then he had hated everyone and everything.

Often when he came home drunk at night, he would kick his dog to get him off the porch. In the process, the dog would bark, growl, and try to bite him. Reeling and rocking under the influence of alcohol, Leonard would chase the dog around a table on the porch.

Soon his wife would get into the fray. They would curse each other and fight. Eventually, he would kick the dog off the porch, scattering chairs and flower pots in all directions.

"But the night I received Christ," he relates, "I was so filled with love that I think even the dog sensed I was different. He raised himself on his belly and crawled toward me, then lay down on the same feet that had kicked him all the other nights."

Take the Step

Agape love frequently expresses itself as a flow of compassion. Jesus said, "Rivers of living water shall flow from the inmost being of anyone who believes in me" (John 7:38, TLB). Compassion is one of these rivers. It is a gentle stream of tenderness and concern for another person's need. Such love compelled Jesus to feed the hungry, comfort the sorrowing, heal the sick, teach the multitude, and raise the dead.

Most of us at some time in our lives have experienced this flow of love toward someone.

Perhaps you felt it while washing dishes, working on the job, driving down the freeway, or sitting in a classroom. You couldn't explain it, but your impulse was to do something special for that person.

I encourage you to take the first step; start loving by faith and follow that flow. It is God's compassion streaming toward the one in need. The tug of love within you means that He is filling you with godly compassion and that He has chosen you to minister to that individual.

Ask God to manifest His tender compassion through you in some way today. As you pray, ask Him to lay someone on your heart. When you sense God's love flowing through you to that individual, find out his need and begin ministering to that need. By following the leading of God's Spirit, you can help those whom the Lord has prepared for His transforming touch, and you will become part of His miraculous provision. When God leads you to help someone, He will enable you to do what He leads you to do (Philippians 4:13; 1 Thessalonians 5:24).

A Japanese magazine has a picture of a butterfly on one of its pages. Its color is a dull gray until warmed by one's hand. The touch of a hand causes the special inks in the printing to react, and the dull gray is transformed into a flashing rainbow of color.

What other things can be thus changed by the warmth of your interest and agape love? Your family? Your church? Your city? This hurting world is hungry for the touch of someone who cares—who really cares! Through God's agape kind of love, you can be that someone.

Make a List

But what about those who seem unlikable? People with whom you may have difficulty getting along? Individuals whose attitudes rub you the wrong way? I encourage you to make a list of people you do not like and begin to love them by faith. Perhaps you will place yourself on the list. Have you thought of applying the truths of 1 Corinthians 13 to yourself by faith? Ask God to help you see yourself as He sees you. You have no reason to dislike yourself when your Creator has already forgiven you and demonstrated His unconditional love by dying for you!

If Christ is in you, you are complete because Christ Himself is perfect love, perfect peace, perfect patience, perfect kindness. He is all goodness, and He is in you!

Whenever Satan tries to attack you by reminding you of sins that you have already confessed or by magnifying your weaknesses and shortcomings, claim in faith the forgiveness and righteousness of God, and thank Him that, on the authority of His Word, you do not have to be intimidated by Satan's accusation. Thank God that you are His child and that your sins are forgiven. Thank God that Satan has no control over you except that which is allowed by God. Then cast this care on the Lord as we are commanded to do in 1 Peter 5:7.

Perhaps your boss, a fellow employee, your spouse, your children, or your father or mother is on the list of those whom you will love by faith. Pray for each person. Ask the Holy Spirit to fill you with Christ's love for all of them. Then, seek to meet with them as you draw upon God's limitless, inexhaustible, overwhelming love for them by faith. Expect God to work through you! Watch Him use your smile, your words, your patience to express His love for each individual.

Love by faith every one of your "enemies"—everyone who angers you, ignores you, bores you, or frustrates you. People are waiting to be loved with God's love.

A homemaker who, through a long, cold winter, had seen her family through mumps, measles, a broken nose, three new teeth for the baby, and countless other difficulties, reached the point where these pressures and demands became too much for her. Finally, on her knees, she began to protest, "Oh Lord! I have so much to do!" But imagine her surprise when she heard herself say, "Oh Lord! I have so much to love!" You will never run out of opportunities to love by faith.

Remember, the agape kind of love is an act of the will, not just an emotion. You love *by faith*. By faith, you can claim God's love step by step, person by person.

"The fruit of the Spirit is love…" Like fruit, love grows. Producing fruit requires a seed, then a flower, then pollination, then warm sun and refreshing rains, and even some contrary winds. Similarly in daily life, your love will be warmed by joy, watered by tears, and spread by the winds of circumstances. God uses all that you experience to work His will in your life. He is the one who makes your love grow. It is a continual, ever-increasing process. As Paul says, "May the Lord make your love to grow and overflow to each other and to everyone else..." (1 Thessalonians 3:12, TLB).

Let Love Motivate You

*N*ow, how does loving by faith motivate you to engage in aggressive personal evangelism and contribute to the fulfillment of the Great Commission?

When you begin to truly love God by faith with all of your heart, soul, mind, and strength and to love your neighbors as yourself, you will begin to see people as God sees them—as individuals of great worth, as those for whom Christ died. As a result, we will be motivated by the same love that constrained the apostle Paul who said, "Everywhere we go we talk about Christ to all who will listen" (Colossians 1:28, TLB).

Love, God's kind of love, causes the Great Commission to become a personal responsibility and privilege. When non-Christians observe believers not only saying that they love one another, but also proving it by their actions, they, like their first-century counterparts, will marvel at "how they love one another" and will be drawn to receive and worship our Savior with us.

How exciting it is to have such a dynamic, joyful force available to us! And it all comes from our loving Savior, Jesus Christ, who explicitly promises in His Word all that you need. You need not guess, nor hope, nor wish. You can claim this love by faith, right now, on the basis of God's command to love and His promise to answer whenever you pray for anything according to His will.

Why not make this prayer your own:

Lord, You would never have commanded me to love if You had not intended to enable me to do so. Therefore, right now, on the authority of Your command for me to love and on the authority of Your promise to answer if I ask anything according to Your will, I personally claim Your love—the 1 Corinthians 13 kind of love—for You, for all people, and for myself. Amen.

N O T E

Remember, *How You Can Love By Faith* is a transferable concept. You can master it by reading it six times; then pass it on to others as our Lord commands us in Matthew 28:20, "Teach these new disciples to obey all the commands I have given you" (TLB). The apostle Paul encouraged us to do the same: "The things you have heard me say in the presence of many witnesses entrust to reliable men who will also be qualified to teach others" (2 Timothy 2:2).

Study Guide

Self-Study Guide

1. How would you explain the difference among eros, phileo, and agape love? (See pages 9,10.)

2. What is unconditional love? How do you show this kind of love to others? (See pages 13–16.)

3. What does Romans 8:35–39 tell us about God's love?

4. Is the depth of God's love real to you? If so, what affect does that realization have on your life? If not, what can you do to increase your realization of His love?

5. How would you obey the command of John 13:34?

6. How do 1 John 3:16–18 and 4:16–21 define real love?

7. How could you express love in the following situations?

   a. At home

   b. At school

   c. At work

   d. At church

   e. At a sporting event

8. Why is it important to love yourself? How do you do this? What often keeps a person from loving himself? How does this affect his love for others? (See pages 24,25.)

9. How and why is love powerful enough to overcome prejudice, hatred, rebellion, anger, fear, or jealousy? (See page 24.)

10. Why do you feel love? (See Romans 5:5.)

11. How can you claim God's love? Why is faith important in love? (See pages 27,28.)

12. What resources can you cling to when you find it difficult to love someone?

    a. 1 Peter 5:7

    b. Philippians 4:13

    c. Colossians 3:2,13

    d. 1 Thessalonians 3:12,13

13. How can you relate the promise in 1 John 5:14,15 to claiming God's power to love others by faith? How does it relate to your own involvement in personal evangelism?

14. Make a list of people you do not like and begin to love them by faith. Ask the Holy Spirit to fill you with Christ's love for each of them. Pray for each person. Think of ways you can demonstrate Christ's love to them this week.

Group Discussion Questions

1. List and discuss the characteristics of God's love found in 1 Corinthians 13. Name a synonym for or give a short description of each characteristic. Share what each quality means to you.

2. Discuss ways in which the church as a body of Christian believers can express its love for God and one another.

3. Have each member of your group share about a person in their lives whom they consider a "neighbor." In what way can you show love to that person?

4. Most of us have at least one weakness in our lives that we find difficult to love. Share this concern (if appropriate) with your group. How does God's love apply to loving yourself in this area?

5. Think of an occasion when you had to claim God's power to love your enemy. Share what happened. If there is someone in your life now who seems unlovable, what will you do this week to change that situation?

6. What are the basic elements of the command given to believers in Matthew 22:36–40? Share what each element means to you.

7. What roles do God's command, His promise, and your will play in loving by faith? (See 1 John 5:14,15.)

8. Loving is a growth process. Share some areas in which God is challenging you to love by faith today.

Fasting & Prayer

In 1994, I felt led by God to undergo a 40-day fast. During that time, God impressed on me that He was going to send a great spiritual awakening to America, and that this revival would be preceded by a time of spiritual preparation through repentance, with a special emphasis on fasting and prayer. In 2 Chronicles 7:14, God gives us a promise of hope that involves repentance:

> *If my people, who are called by my name, will humble themselves and pray and seek my face and turn from their wicked ways, then will I hear from heaven and will forgive their sin and will heal their land.*

Fasting is the only spiritual discipline that meets all the conditions of 2 Chronicles 7:14. When a person fasts, he humbles himself; he has more time to pray; he has more time to seek God's face, and certainly he would turn from all known sin. One could read the Bible, pray, or witness for Christ without repenting of his sins. But one cannot enter into a genuine fast with a pure heart and pure motive and not meet the conditions of this passage.

Because of this promise, God has led me to pray that at least two million North Americans will fast and pray for forty days for an awakening in America and the fulfillment of the Great Commission. As millions of Christians rediscover the power of fasting as it relates to the holy life, prayer, and witnessing, they will come alive. Out of this great move of God's Spirit will come the revival for which we have all prayed so long, resulting in the fulfillment of the Great Commission.

I invite you to become one of the two million who will fast and pray for forty days. Also, I encourage you to attend the Fasting & Prayer gatherings held each year. If you feel God leading you to participate, please let us know on the Response Form. For more information, see the Resources or call (800) 888-FAST.

Other Resources by Bill Bright

Resources for Fasting and Prayer

The Coming Revival: America's Call to Fast, Pray, and "Seek God's Face." This inspiring yet honest book explains how the power of fasting and prayer by millions of God's people can usher in a mighty spiritual revival and lift His judgment on America. *The Coming Revival* can equip Christians, their churches, and our nation for the greatest spiritual awakening since the first century.

7 Basic Steps to Successful Fasting and Prayer. This handy booklet gives practical steps to undertaking and completing a fast, suggests a plan for prayer, and offers an easy-to-follow daily nutritional schedule.

Preparing for the Coming Revival: How to Lead a Successful Fasting and Prayer Gathering. In this easy-to-use handbook, the author presents step-by-step instructions on how to plan and conduct a fasting and prayer gathering in your church or community. The book also contains creative ideas for teaching group prayer and can be used for a small group or large gatherings.

The Transforming Power of Fasting and Prayer. This follow-up book to *The Coming Revival* includes stirring accounts of Christians who have participated in the fasting and prayer movement that is erupting across the country.

Resources for Group and Individual Study

Five Steps of Christian Growth. This five-lesson Bible study will help group members be sure that they are a Christian, learn what it means to grow as a Christian, experience the joy of God's love and forgiveness, and discover how to be filled with the Holy Spirit. Leader's and Study Guides are available.

Five Steps to Sharing Your Faith. This Bible study is designed to help Christians develop a lifestyle of introducing others to Jesus Christ. With these step-by-step lessons, believers can learn how to share their faith with confidence through the power of the Holy Spirit. Leader's and Study Guides are available.

Five Steps to Knowing God's Will. This five-week Bible study includes detailed information on applying the Sound Mind Principle to discover God's will. Both new and more mature Christians will find clear instructions useful for every aspect of decision-making. Leader's and Study Guides are available.

Five Steps to Making Disciples. This effective Bible study can be used for one-on-one discipleship, leadership evangelism training in your church, or a neighborhood Bible study group. Participants will learn how to begin a Bible study to disciple new believers as well as more mature Christians. Leader's and Study Guides are available.

Ten Basic Steps Toward Christian Maturity. These time-tested Bible studies offer a simple way to understand the basics of the Christian faith and provide believers with a solid foundation for growth. The product of many years of extensive development, the studies have been used by thousands. Leader's and Study Guides are available.

Introduction: The Uniqueness of Jesus
Step 1: The Christian Adventure
Step 2: The Christian and the Abundant Life
Step 3: The Christian and the Holy Spirit
Step 4: The Christian and Prayer
Step 5: The Christian and the Bible
Step 6: The Christian and Obedience
Step 7: The Christian and Witnessing
Step 8: The Christian and Giving

Step 9: Exploring the Old Testament
Step 10: Exploring the New Testament

A Handbook for Christian Maturity. This book combines the *Ten Basic Steps* Study Guides in one handy volume. The lessons can be used for daily devotions or with groups of all sizes.

Ten Basic Steps Leader's Guide. This book contains teacher's helps for the entire *Ten Basic Steps* Bible Study series. The lessons include opening and closing prayers, objectives, discussion starters, and suggested answers to the questions.

Resources for Christian Growth

Transferable Concepts. This series of time-tested messages teaches the principles of abundant Christian life and ministry. These "back-to-the-basics" resources help Christians grow toward greater spiritual maturity and fulfillment and live victorious Christian lives. These messages, available in book format and on video or audio cassette, include:

How You Can Be Sure You Are a Christian
How You Can Experience God's Love and Forgiveness
How You Can Be Filled With the Spirit
How You Can Walk in the Spirit
How You Can Be a Fruitful Witness
How You Can Introduce Others to Christ
How You Can Help Fulfill the Great Commission
How You Can Love By Faith
How You Can Pray With Confidence
How You Can Experience the Adventure of Giving

A Man Without Equal. This book explores the unique birth, life, teachings, death, and resurrection of Jesus Christ and shows how He continues to change the way we live and think today. Available in book and video formats.

Life Without Equal. This inspiring book shows how Christians can experience pardon, purpose, peace, and power for living the Christian life. The book also explains how to release Christ's resurrection power to help change the world.

Have You Made the Wonderful Discovery of the Spirit-Filled Life? This booklet shows how you can discover the reality of the Spirit-filled life and live in moment-by-moment dependence on God.

The Holy Spirit: Key to Supernatural Living. This booklet helps you enter into the Spirit-filled life and explains how you can experience power and victory.

Promises: A Daily Guide to Supernatural Living. These 365 devotionals will help you remain focused on God's great love and faithfulness by reading and meditating on His promises each day. You will find your faith growing as you get to know our God and Savior better.

Resources for Evangelism

Witnessing Without Fear. This best-selling, Gold Medallion book offers simple hands-on, step-by-step coaching on how to share your faith with confidence. The chapters give specific answers to questions people most often encounter in witnessing and provide a proven method for sharing your faith.

Reaching Your World Through Witnessing Without Fear. This six-session video provides the resources needed to sensitively share the gospel effectively. Each session begins with a captivating dramatic vignette to help viewers apply the training. Available in individual study and group packages.

These and other products from Campus Crusade are available at www.campuscrusade.org or by calling **(800) 827-2788** *(within U.S.) or* **(770) 631-9940** *(outside U.S.).*

Have You Heard of the Four Spiritual Laws? This booklet is one of the most effective evangelistic tools ever developed. It presents a clear explanation of the gospel of Jesus Christ, which helps you open a conversation easily and share your faith with confidence.

Would You Like to Know God Personally? Based on the *Four Spiritual Laws*, this booklet uses a friendly, conversational format to present four principles for establishing a personal relationship with God.

Jesus and the Intellectual. Drawing from the works of notable scholars who affirm their faith in Jesus Christ, this booklet shows that Christianity is based on irrefutable historic facts. Good for sharing with unbelievers and new Christians.

A Great Adventure. Written as from one friend to another, this booklet explains how to know God personally and experience peace, joy, meaning, and fulfillment in life.

Resources by Vonette Bright

The Joy of Hospitality: Fun Ideas for Evangelistic Entertaining. Co-written with Barbara Ball, this practical book tells how to share your faith through hosting barbecues, coffees, holiday parties, and other events in your home.

The Joy of Hospitality Cookbook. Filled with uplifting Scriptures and quotations, this cookbook contains hundreds of delicious recipes, hospitality tips, sample menus, and family traditions that are sure to make your entertaining a memorable and eternal success. Co-written with Barbara Ball.

Beginning Your Journey of Joy. This adaptation of the *Four Spiritual Laws* speaks in the language of today's women and offers a slightly feminine approach to sharing God's love with your neighbors, friends, and family members.

 BILL BRIGHT was the founder and president of Campus Crusade for Christ International, the world's largest Christian ministry which serves people in 191 countriesthrough a staff of 26,000 full-time employees and more than 225,000 trained volunteers.

Dr. Bright did graduate studies at Princeton and Fuller Theological seminaries and was the recipient of five honorary doctorates as well as many national and international awards. In 1996 Bright was presented with the prestigious Templeton Prize for Progress in Religion, for his work with fasting and prayer. Worth more than $1 million, the Templeton Prize is the world's largest financial annual award. Bright donated all of his prize money to causes promoting the spiritual benefits of fasting and prayer.

In 2000, Bright received the first Lifetime Achievement Award from his alma mater, Northeastern State University. In that same year, Bright and his wife were given the Lifetime Inspiration Award from Religious Heritage of America Foundation. Additionally, he received the Lifetime Achievement Award from both the National Association of Evangelicals and the Evangelical Christian Publishers Association. In 2002, Dr. Bright was inducted into the National Religious Broadcasters Hall of Fame. He authored over 100 books and publications committed to helping fulfill the Great Commission.

Before Dr. Bright went home to be with the Lord on July 19, 2003, he established Bright Media Foundation to promote and extend his written legacy to future generations.

Response Form

○ I have received Jesus Christ as my Savior and Lord as a result of reading this book.

○ I am a new Christian and want to know Christ better and experience the abundant Christian life.

○ I want to be one of the two million people who will join you in forty days of fasting and prayer for revival.

○ I have completed an extended or forty-day fast with prayer and am enclosing my written testimony to encourage and bless others.

○ Please send me *free* information on staff and ministry opportunities with Campus Crusade for Christ.

○ Please send me *free* information about other books, booklets, audio cassettes, and videos by Bill and Vonette Bright.

_____
NAME

_____
ADDRESS

_____
CITY   STATE   ZIP

_____
COUNTRY

Please check the appropriate box(es), clip, and mail this form in an envelope to:

> Campus Crusade for Christ
> 375 Hwy 74 South, Suite A
> Peachtree City, GA 30269

Or send E-mail to nlrrep@campuscrusade.org. Visit our website at www.campuscrusade.org.